THE PENAN
PEOPLE OF THE BORNEO JUNGLE

THE PENAN

PEOPLE OF THE BORNEO JUNGLE

by

ALEXANDRA SIY

DILLON PRESS
New York

Maxwell Macmillan Canada
Toronto

Maxwell Macmillan International
New York Oxford Singapore Sydney

ACKNOWLEDGMENTS

The author would like to thank Dr. Peter Brosius of the University of Georgia for sharing his knowledge, experiences, and wonderful photographs. Also thanks to Dr. Wade Davis for his help. Additional thanks are extended to Bruno Manser, Anthony Dixon, Ramond Abin (Sahabat Alam Malaysia), Ursula Odermatt (World Wide Fund for Nature), and Polly Mathewson (Survival International).

The author would like to thank Thom Henley for sharing the three Penan legends: *How the Penan Came to Be, The Boy Who Didn't Share,* and *The Legend of the Slow Loris.* Thom Henley heard the first two stories from Bruno Manser and the third from Anderson Mutang Tuo. The statement made by Dawat Lupung on page 25 is reprinted with the gracious permission of the publisher, Western Canada Wilderness Committee, from *Penan: Voice for the Borneo Rain Forest,* by Wade Davis and Thom Henley, copyright 1990.

PHOTO CREDITS

Cover courtesy of Survival International/Payne
Back cover courtesy of Thom Henley
Thom Henley: title page, 17, 19, 24; Peter Brosius: 10, 14, 21, 27, 29, 31, 33, 39, 41, 48, 50, 55; Survival International/Payne: 28, 35, 44; World Wide Fund for Nature/Mattias Klum: 60.

Book design by Carol Matsuyama

LIBRARY OF CONGRESS CATALOGING-IN-PUBLICATION DATA

Siy, Alexandra.
    The Penan : people of the Borneo jungle / by Alexandra Siy. – 1st ed.
       p. cm. – (Global villages)
    Includes bibliographical references (p.) and index.
    Summary: Describes the way of life of the Penan, the last remaining group of nomadic hunter-gatherers in Borneo, and explains how their culture is being threatened by the loss of their rain forests to foreign logging interests.
    ISBN 0-87518-552-5
    1. Penan (Bornean people)–Juvenile literature. I. Title. II. Series.
DS595.2.P44S58 1993
959.8'3–dc20   93-10007

Dillon Press
Macmillan Publishing Company
866 Third Avenue
New York, NY 10022

Maxwell Macmillan Canada, Inc.
1200 Eglinton Avenue East
Suite 200
Don Mills, Ontario M3C 3N1

Macmillan Publishing Company is part of the Maxwell Communication Group of Companies.

First edition

Printed in the United States of America
10 9 8 7 6 5 4 3 2 1

CONTENTS

INTRODUCTION

As the 1990s draw to a close, we look forward to not only a new century but a new millennium. What will the next thousand years bring for the planet earth and its people? And what aspects of our ancient past will we retain on our journey into a new time, a new world?

Today the world is already a vastly different place from what our great-grandparents would have imagined. People from distant parts of the planet can communicate within seconds. In less than 24 hours, you can fly around the world. Thanks to these and other remarkable advances in technology, the world has become a "global village."

In a sense, the peoples of the earth are no longer strangers, but neighbors. As we meet our "neighbors," we learn that now, more than ever before, our lives are intertwined. Indeed, our survival may depend on one another.

In a small corner of Southeast Asia, on the island of Borneo, a people have lived for generations in much the same ways as their ancestors. Known as the Penan, they are among the last hunter-gatherers on earth. They lead a wandering, nomadic life in the tropical rain forests of Sarawak. Despite changes brought to them by missionaries in the last half of this century, the Penan have held on to much of their traditional culture and heritage. In the last decade, however, the Penan have been forced to fight a battle for survival: Their rain forest is being logged by foreigners at an alarming rate. Experts predict that if logging continues at its current pace, all of Sarawak's tropical rain forests will be gone by the year 2000.

This is the story of the Penan and their struggle to save their rain-forest home. It is also the story of all the people who make up the global village, for what happens to the Penan affects us all.

FAST FACTS

CULTURE
Hunting, gathering, and trading in the tropical rain forests of Borneo.

HUMAN HISTORY
Anthropologists do not know how long the Penan have lived in Borneo's rain forests but believe they have survived there for thousands of years. Prolonged contact with Westerners began in the 1800s during the rule of James Brooke.

NATURAL HISTORY
Borneo's rain forests are part of the ancient tropical rain forests that once blanketed nearly all of Southeast Asia. Southeast Asian rain forests are the oldest on earth–at least 150 million years.

GEOGRAPHY
Most Penan live in Sarawak, a state in the Federation of Malaysia. Sarawak lies on the northwestern coast of the island of Borneo in Southeast Asia. The Penan are forest dwellers, living inland near the headwaters of the Baram, Limbang, and Balui rivers.

CLIMATE
Wet, averaging 200 inches of rain a year. Daytime temperatures average 80°F and the humidity is almost always more than 80 percent.

GLOBAL IMPORTANCE
The Penan are some of the last hunter-gatherers left on earth. Their rain-forest homeland is extremely rich in biological diversity. The largest tropical hardwood trees in the world grow there. The Penan knowledge of rain-forest plants is immense and could benefit modern medicine.

CURRENT STATUS

The rain forests in Sarawak are being logged for tropical timber at an alarming rate. Foreign countries, such as Japan, finance the logging industry. Experts predict that all of Sarawak's primary rain forests will be gone by the year 2000 if the logging continues at its current pace.

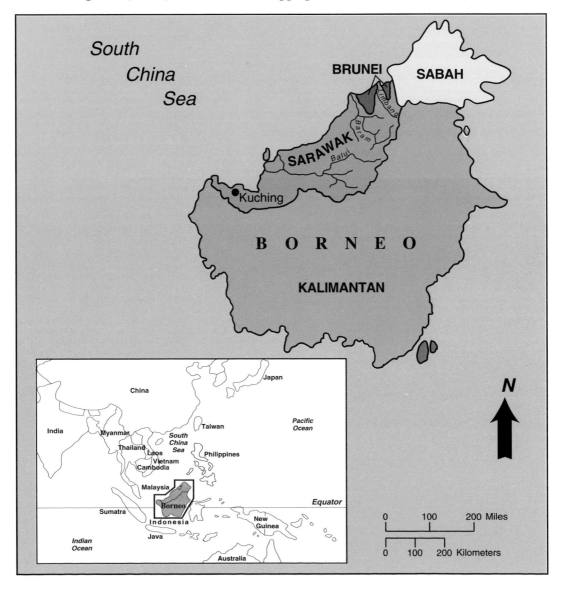

CHAPTER ONE

THE PENAN PLACE

Once the island of Borneo was covered entirely by rain forests. Within the jungles were hidden wonders: soaring mist-covered mountains, emerald rivers, dramatic rock pinnacles, and gigantic caves. In these places all kinds of creatures lived–long-tailed macaques, wreathed hornbills, orangutans, green pit vipers, fruit-eating fish, and millions of screeching cicadas–each interconnected and dependent on the rain forest for life. People, too, were part of this delicate balance.

People still live in Borneo's rain forest. Among them are the Penan, and this is the story they tell about their origins.

HOW THE PENAN CAME TO BE

Long ago the forest was filled with trees so beautiful that they couldn't help but fall in love with one another. Like the arms of lovers in a tender embrace, long climbing vines twined about one another. Giant strangler fig trees grew long root "legs" and branch "arms" around host trees as if in a passionate hug. The entire rain forest was interconnected in an act of eternal love.

When the very first man and woman stood alone in the forest, they were inspired by the love embrace of those powerful and beautiful trees. In the shade of the forest, they imitated the

The Borneo rain forest, home of the Penan

trees, and soon children were born. These were the first people–
the Penan.

ANCIENT FORESTS

The Penan live in the dense jungles surrounding the headwaters
of Borneo's big rivers. This region is part of Sarawak, a state in
northwestern Borneo.

Located in the South China Sea, Borneo is the third largest
island in the world. Borneo's rain forests are ancient.

Many millions of years ago, when the earth was warmer
than it is now, rain forests blanketed most of the planet. But
about 2.5 million years ago global temperatures dropped and the
northern parts of Asia, Europe, and North America were covered
with glaciers. Much of the water on earth was frozen in these
massive ice sheets, and the world became drier. As a result,
tropical rain forests shrank in size, and some disappeared completely–replaced by seasonal forests and grasslands.

However, scientists believe that Borneo's tropical forests
continued to **evolve** despite the drier and colder world climate.
Straddling the equator and surrounded by ocean, Borneo remained one of the warmest and wettest places on earth.

ANCIENT PEOPLE

Anthropologists think that people have lived in Southeast Asia
for more than one million years. In Sarawak's Great Cave at

Niah, human remains were uncovered that date back many thousands of years. No one knows, however, if any of the **indigenous,** or native, people who live in the Borneo rain forests are related to those ancient cave dwellers.

Scientists do believe that the ancestors of many of Borneo's native people migrated to the island from other parts of Southeast Asia, beginning about 4,000 years ago. The origins of the Penan, though, who live in small groups, or bands, scattered in the forest, are less clear. The Penan, however, believe their ancestors were the first people to live in their part of the Borneo rain forest. They say, "This land is our origin."

BORNEO IN HISTORY

Sometime around 500 B.C., Indian spice merchants established trading posts on many of the islands in Southeast Asia. Traders from Persia and China followed.

It was not long before many tropical products became valuable trade items. In Borneo, tree **resins** (for ship varnish), beeswax, edible bird nests, scent glands of wild animals (for perfumes), fragrant wood, and cinnabar (a bright red mineral), were gathered by forest-dwelling hunter-gatherers and exchanged for material items with coastal natives. The coastal people then traded these forest products with Indian, Arab, and Chinese merchants, who transported them to foreign countries in Asia and the West.

A Penan family at home in their rain-forest camp

The first European ships to arrive in the region belonged to the Portuguese in the early 1500s. The Spanish soon followed. The Dutch arrived in the early 1600s and their influence began to grow. By the 1800s the Dutch controlled the southern three-fourths of the island, although they had little influence on the native peoples living deep in the rain forests.

In 1841, James Brooke, an officer of the British East India Company, made a deal with the Sultan of Brunei, a small kingdom on the island's northwest coast. In exchange for land surrounding the Sarawak River, Brooke agreed to make peace among hostile tribes and stop pirates from attacking merchant ships off the coast.

Brooke built forts along the region's waterways, thus preventing warring tribes from paddling into one another's territories. These forts eventually became principal cities, among them Sarawak's capital, Kuching. Brooke took over large tracts of land in northwestern Borneo. These areas are now part of the 48,000 square miles of land that make up present-day Sarawak.

History remembers Brooke as a benevolent ruler. He admired the indigenous people and worked to protect the tribes living deep in the jungles from outsiders. He set up rules that guaranteed fair prices for the inlanders when they bartered with the tribes living downriver and along the coast.

Brooke's descendants ruled Sarawak for more than 100 years before **ceding** the country to England in 1946. In 1963, Sarawak gained its independence from Great Britain and joined the newly formed Federation of Malaysia.

THE PENAN PLACE

Six major rivers flow across Borneo into the sea. These rivers are fed by hundreds of streams that drain from the mountains in the center of the island. Today, most Penan live in the hilly territory inland from the Baram, Limbang, and Balui rivers in Sarawak.

The island of Borneo is divided into four regions that belong to three different countries. Sarawak and neighboring Sabah to the north are the two eastern states of Malaysia, the rest of which lies across the South China Sea to the west. The tiny oil-rich sultanate of Brunei is wedged into the northern coast of Sarawak. South of these states, and occupying most of the island, is Kalimantan. This region was controlled by the Dutch until 1949 and is now a province of the island nation of Indonesia.

The yearly average rainfall in Sarawak is about 200 inches. During the daytime the average temperature is 80°F, and the humidity is almost always more than 80 percent. Because Borneo is on the equator, the length of the days and nights are equal throughout the year. Unchanging daylight, along with the constant warm and wet climate, gives the impression that Sarawak is a land without seasons.

Yet the Penan place is always changing, its rhythms the life cycles of rain-forest plants and animals. Flowering, fruiting, decaying–pregnancy, birth, and death–are its "seasons." The Penan are deeply connected to, and dependent on, these rhythms. These ancient people are a part of the great diversity of life that thrives in the rain forest.

BIOLOGICAL DIVERSITY

Borneo's forests are extremely rich in **biological diversity**. Biological diversity refers to the variety of plants and animals living in a specific place. There are many reasons why Borneo's forests

A vast variety of plants thrive in the hot and humid rain forest. The Penan have learned to use many for foods and medicines.

have so many different kinds, or **species**, of plants and animals. Most obvious is the constant warm and humid weather, which provides favorable growing conditions year-round. Another is the actual structure of the forest: Its huge trees tower more than 200 feet above the ground and create a multitude of living spaces for millions of creatures.

Borneo's **geological** history also helped the forest develop a rich variety of life. During several periods in its ancient past, the island was connected to and then isolated from the mainland of Southeast Asia. When sea levels were low during the earth's ice ages, a bridge of land connected Borneo to the mainland. Species migrated across the bridge. As time passed and the sea levels rose again, these species remained isolated on the island.

These periods of connection and isolation resulted in the evolution of many **endemic** species–those found nowhere else in the world. The Borneo gibbon, for example, is one of the smallest apes on earth and lives only in the treetops of the Borneo rain forest. And 38 other species of mammals, 30 species of birds, and about 10,000 species of plants are native only to the island of Borneo.

CULTURAL DIVERSITY

The people of Borneo are also diverse and unique. The Penan are one of the 26 tribes of indigenous peoples collectively known as Dayaks. In Sarawak these tribes account for about 50 percent of the population.

Each tribe follows its own traditions and speaks its own language. Most Dayak tribes live in wooden **longhouses** in settled villages, where they practice **shifting cultivation**.

In the past, several of these tribes were **nomadic**, which means that they traveled from place to place in the forest in search of food. They were hunter-gatherers, surviving on the food they hunted or gathered from the forest. Today the Penan are the last of Sarawak's nomads.

This young orangutan is just one of the many different kinds of animals that live in the Borneo rain forest..

PENAN TODAY

Twenty-five years ago almost all of the Penan were nomadic hunter-gatherers. Of the 10,000 Penan living in Sarawak today, only 400 people continue the wandering life of their ancestors. A large number are semi-settled, living part of the time in small, scattered villages.

These semi-settled Penan still depend on the rain forest for most of their food and material needs. Although they may grow rice and **cassava**, they still go hunting in the forest every day. Yet, farming has proved difficult for the Penan, who have no traditional knowledge of cultivation, crops, and growing seasons. A few families have given up farming and returned to the jungle.

Today the Penan have lost control of their land. Now the state government of Sarawak controls the rain forest and decides where indigenous people may live. It also decides what parts of the forest will be chopped down for timber.

Less than 1 percent of Sarawak's rain forests have been set aside for indigenous peoples. And the policy that determines what tribes will receive a "communal forest" doesn't respect the different life-styles of the peoples. A communal forest is granted only after a native group has farmed the land, built permanent houses, and made a formal application to the government.

This presents the Penan, who survive mostly by hunting

An elder and child. The Penan, one of the last groups of hunter-gatherers on earth, continue to live as their ancestors have for thousands of years.

and gathering, with an impossible situation: To establish a legal and recognized homeland, they must give up their traditional way of life.

DESTRUCTION OF THE FORESTS

The Penan believe they have a right to keep their traditions and to live in the same ways as their ancestors. For centuries the rain forest has provided them with everything they have needed for survival. Now the forests of Sarawak are falling to chain saws and bulldozers.

The lumber is sold to the industrialized nations of Japan, Taiwan, and Korea, where it is processed into plywood, hollow-core doors, and cheap furniture. Some of these products are sold in the United States under the name *luan*.

Between 1963 and 1985, 30 percent of the rain forests in Sarawak were logged. Today, Sarawak exports almost one-half of all the tropical timber in the world. Some experts predict that Sarawak's ancient rain forests will be gone by the year 2000 if logging continues at its current pace.

THE GLOBAL VILLAGE

Today many people have come to understand that the earth is a **global village**. Like neighbors in a small town, nations in the world are closely connected to and dependent on one another.

Industrialized nations have always needed to look beyond

their borders for natural resources, such as oil and minerals. They found them in less developed nations, which they often made into colonies. Today a modern form of **colonialism** continues. Outsiders seeking an area's resources continue to hurt native inhabitants and their environments.

More and more, however, people living in industrialized nations are beginning to take action. They are boycotting certain companies, writing letters in support of indigenous peoples, and using resources more thoughtfully.

Indigenous people, too, are speaking out. They are demanding that governments respect their rights to their traditional homelands. They have asked to be represented in the United Nations. Although the United Nations declared 1993 as the Year of the World's Indigenous People, it has done little to help native peoples.

Some scientists believe that the rain forests will be preserved only if the rights of the native peoples who live in them are respected.

CHAPTER TWO

HUNTERS AND GATHERERS

"This forest, we want to preserve it, because we have a good life here. We live by getting palm heart, by getting sago. We eat different types of animals. We go out with blowpipe, get something, return . . . ah! Content to eat, content with life.

"From large trees much fruit falls to the ground–the food of pigs, the food of deer, food of all animals in the forest. If the land is preserved like this, all the hornbills, all the pigs, all animals are happy to eat the fruits of the trees.

"We, too, eat the fruits of this land. There are many medicines, many hunting poisons here in the forest. But if the company comes, this is finished–it is destroyed. That is why we need to save this land, a big piece of land. We are content to stay on this land, to make our shelters in this forest. This is a good life."

–Dawat Lupung, a Penan

A HUNTER'S TOOLS: SPEARS, BLOWPIPES, AND POISONED DARTS

The Penan hunt a wide variety of animals, including wild bearded pigs (*babui*), monkeys, apes, deer, birds, squirrels, and bears. Large animals, such as *babui*, are killed with spears.

A Penan hunter alert for any signs of game in the forest

Monkeys, birds, and other animals that dwell high in the forest **canopy** are killed with poisoned darts fired from *keleputs,* or blowpipes.

A hunter spends several weeks making a *keleput* out of materials he finds in the forest. First he cuts a six-foot piece of hardwood from the *nyagang* tree. The barrel of the gun is made by pushing a long iron drill into the wood. Iron drills have been available through trade for at least 50 years. Before iron drills were available to the Penan, their ancestors fashioned blowpipes from bamboo.

When the barrel of the blowpipe is completely drilled, the hunter rounds the outside of the weapon with a *nahan,* or steel knife. He "sands" it to a smooth finish using *bekkela* leaves. Finally he lashes an *atap,* an iron blade, to the end. Now his finished blowpipe is also a spear.

Blowpipe darts are made from *nibong* palm stems and carved into perfectly straight arrows–about ten inches in length. Some dart tips are sharpened. These are *tahats* and are used for killing small game, such as birds and squirrels.

A metal tip, made from an old tin can, is fastened to the end of an arrow to make a *belat. The belat* is used for hunting large animals, such as deer and monkeys. Before metal was available, the Penan made arrow tips out of bone.

Both kinds of darts are dipped into *tajem,* a poison prepared from the sap of the *ipoh* tree. The process of making *tajem* is

A hunter uses a long iron drill to make the barrel of a blowpipe from a piece of wood.

similar to tapping sap from a maple tree to produce maple syrup. The hunter makes a V-shaped slash in the bark of the tree and collects the dripping **latex** in a bamboo cylinder. The latex is

Coating the dart tips with sticky tajem, *a poison made from the sap of a tree*

heated over a fire until it becomes thick and sticky. The tips of the darts are coated with the syrup and stored in a *tello,* or bamboo quiver.

HUNTING . . .

The Penan hunt in small groups, in pairs, or alone, depending on the kind of animal they are seeking. Large animals, such as wild pigs and deer, are tracked by groups of hunters and their dogs. The Penan prize wild pig meat the most because it is high in

After several hours of quiet tracking, a hunter spears a wild pig.

both fat and protein. Cooked pig fat can also be stored for many weeks, even in the warm tropical climate.

Stalking **prey** that live in the trees requires a hunter to be alert and very quiet. When tracking monkeys, a hunter must be able to see everything. He must look into the trees to watch the animals while also watching where he walks. If his movements are heard, the monkeys will make their getaway through the treetops.

When a hunter spots his prey, he quickly loads his *keleput* and aims. He seals his lips around the mouthpiece of the blowpipe and blows hard. The air from his lungs backs up behind a wooden cone that is attached to the base of the dart.

The cone is like a cork in a bottle, sealing the chamber of the blowpipe. Air pressure builds rapidly behind the cone until the dart, with the cone attached, breaks away. Speeding up the barrel and into the air, the dart often travels 100 feet before hitting its target.

Injured prey do not die immediately. It takes 10 to 30 minutes for the deadly *tajem* to take effect. During this time a hunter must follow the animal through the forest until it finally falls dead on the ground.

. . . GATHERING

Hunting provides meat, which is an essential part of the Penan diet. However, hunting is an unpredictable pursuit–sometimes a hunter returns with nothing, sometimes he kills more than enough. A wide variety of fruit, fish, nuts, mushrooms, and leaves gathered from the forest provide the Penan with additional foods.

The Penan eagerly look forward to the annual fruit season, which lasts about two months. They watch and talk about the growth and ripening of the fruit. The Penan say that when the honeybees swarm and the hornbills all fly in one direction, the fruit season is about to begin. Following the bees come the wild pigs, which constantly migrate throughout the

After the kill, a hunter and his young helper work on their catch. Wild pig meat–a rich source of both protein and fat–is greatly prized by the Penan.

rain forest in search of ripe fruit. The fruit season is also the best time of the year for hunting pigs, which are fat from eating fruit.

The Penan eat more than 100 different kinds of fruit and 30 different species of fish. Women lure fruit-eating fish into their waiting nets using stones that make the same size splash as falling fruit. Another way Penan catch fish is by dumping poison made from crushed plants into a slowly moving stream. The fish die and float to the surface.

But more than any other food, the Penan depend on the starch they get from *uvud*–sago palm trees. Sago starch, or *apo*, is their staple, or regular and dependable, food.

PENAN "POTATOES"

The Penan eat sago with wild game like Americans eat potatoes with meat. They know where to go to find sago palms. And they are careful how they take sago to ensure that it continues to flourish in the rain forest–generation after generation.

Sago palms grow in clumps. Because there are sharp spines at the base of the palm, the men must stand on log platforms to reach the upper part of the trunk. They harvest sago by cutting two or three trunks at a time. Cutting the trunk does not kill the tree. The palms will continue to grow and provide sago as long as the roots are left undamaged.

The sago trunks are cut into four-foot sections and carried to the bank of a stream. There, men and boys split each piece lengthwise with an ax. Next the pith, or soft part of the trunk, is chopped out with a mallet.

The women and girls collect the chopped pith, which looks and feels like wet sawdust, and place it on a raised mat. They add a little bit of stream water and trample it until starch oozes onto a collecting mat below.

The starch is sloppy and wet and looks like white mud. Once the starch has settled in a thick layer on the mat, the excess water is poured off. Then the wet starch is cut into chunks and carried back to the camp.

The rest of the water is removed by smoking the starch over a fire. The result is pure starch flour, which the women store in

Harvesting sago: A woman collects the pith of a sago palm tree and places it on a mat. Later, she will add water to the sawdust-like material and trample on it with her feet, producing sago starch.

woven **rattan** bags. The entire process, harvesting trunks and making sago flour, takes one day.

Women make sago flour into a variety of dishes. The simplest meal is a paste made by mixing the flour with water over a fire. Sometimes sago is cooked with pig meat wrapped in leaves–called *gerumut,* it is a Penan favorite.

GIVE AND TAKE

The Penan **economy** has long depended on trade with other Dayak tribes. Today the Penan still barter forest products such as cinnamon bark, rattan, jelutong (wild rubber), garu (incense wood), and dammar (resin) in exchange for cooking pots, knives, matches, salt, tobacco, and clothes.

Rattan products are especially desirable. Rattan is a climbing palm that is harvested by slashing the tough shoots into ten-foot-long pieces. Women wash the rattan in stream water and leave it in the sun to dry. After several weeks of drying, they rub it in sawdust and then bury it in the ground. The whole process can take more than a month, but when finished, the women have a flexible and strong material from which they weave baskets, mats, and bracelets.

Penan women spend a lot of time weaving. A small basket takes two days to make; a large one can require two weeks of work. Mats used for sleeping or for filtering sago take several weeks to complete.

The Penan are known as the best weavers in Borneo. Every item is a work of art, characterized by intricate designs and patterns.

"PROFESSORS" OF THE RAIN FOREST

The Penan are sometimes called the "professors" of the rain forest because their knowledge of the jungle is immense. They know

The Penan have a reputation for being the best weavers in Borneo. Here, a woman quietly makes a beautiful basket.

how to make medicines, insect repellents, hunting and fishing poisons, soaps, and dyes from plants. They craft musical instruments and hunting weapons from wood. The Penan know which trees give the gums and resins used to capture birds and to make burning torches.

The rain forest is their farm, factory, laboratory, store, and home. Their way of life is an art that is not easily learned but mastered only with practice, cooperation, and wisdom.

CHAPTER THREE

THE ART OF LIVING

Once there was a small boy who was learning how to hunt with a *keleput*. But he was still too young to use poisoned darts. He hunted pygmy squirrels and small birds instead of the monkeys, deer, and *babui* sought by the men and older boys.

One day the boy was hunting in the forest alone. Suddenly a *telle,* a pygmy squirrel, darted up a tree to feed on bark fungus. The boy put a dart in his *keleput,* aimed at the squirrel, and blew into the pipe. The dart pierced the squirrel's body and the tiny animal fell dead to the ground.

The boy was very hungry because he hadn't eaten for a couple of days. He eagerly cooked his catch over a small fire. While the meat cooked, the boy made a traditional Penan offering to the animal's spirit. Then he ate the entire squirrel.

When the boy returned home, he told his friends and family how he had killed and eaten the squirrel. He was ashamed because he knew that he had broken the most important rule in his village: He had not shared.

His parents were not angry. Instead they laughed and said, "You need a new name. From now on we'll call you Telle!"

And for the rest of his life, the boy remembered the day that he forgot to share.

TEACHING THE CHILDREN

The Penan say that *sihun,* which means "selfishness," is the most serious crime a member of their community can commit. They teach their children that everything must be shared among all the people. Even a tiny fruit is sliced into enough pieces so that everyone can have a bite. Sharing is so natural among the Penan that in their language there is no word or phrase that means "thank you."

Values such as sharing, along with the skills and knowledge needed to survive in the rain forest, are learned in many ways. Legends and stories sometimes have a message that helps children understand what their society expects of them. Some children, those who live in villages, attend government schools. But traditionally, Penan children did not go to school. They learned everything from their mothers, fathers, aunts, uncles, and grandparents.

Penan children learn the names and uses of hundreds of rain-forest plants and animals. Without compasses or maps, they learn how to navigate through the jungle. And they learn how to start a fire, build a shelter, and make tools.

Boys learn how to make blowpipes, darts, and *tajem* by watching and helping their fathers and grandfathers. They learn to hunt with their friends in the forest. Girls learn to weave by watching and helping their mothers and grandmothers. They gather fruit, nuts, and fish with their friends. Both boys and girls learn how to harvest sago and make flour at a young age. Children play games, too. They climb trees, splash in streams, and slide down muddy slopes.

All children grow up without birthday parties, graduations, or other ceremonies that mark the passage of time. A young person is old enough to marry when he or she has mastered the skills and knowledge needed to support a family–usually at about 16 years of age. Then a young Penan woman and man may simply decide to live together as husband and wife. There is no marriage ceremony.

RESPECT AND STEWARDSHIP

But learning doesn't end when a child becomes an adult. People learn from the elders throughout their lives. Penan elders carry a vast amount of knowledge in their heads and they share this knowledge with their children and grandchildren every day. Elders are highly respected. In Penan society, each person is respected, for each person contributes to the community's success.

The Penan have a concept called *molong,* which means to preserve or to foster. *Molong* is a kind of **stewardship**–a way of taking care of particular fruit trees or clumps of sago. The

A Penan elder relaxes at camp. Elders are highly respected members of the community and are sought after not only for their great store of knowledge, but also for their wonderful stories.

Penan use the resources of the forest wisely, knowing that it provides them with food, water, and shelter. For example, the Penan never cut down or disturb the fruit trees that the wild pigs eat from. This ensures a healthy pig population year after year.

A PLACE CALLED HOME

Nomadic Penan construct huts in the forest made from saplings, or young trees. A roof is made by weaving palm leaves together into a waterproof mat. Floors are built above the ground and look like wooden grates.

The Penan build their temporary villages on hilltops away from streams, where the ground is drier. There they are less likely to be hit by decaying, fallen trees or be swarmed by insects.

Each family builds its own *lamin,* or hut. The construction takes only a few hours. A fire burns inside each *lamin.* The only "furniture" consists of sleeping mats and shelves used for storing a few possessions, such as cooking pots, knives, and hunting weapons. Material things are a burden to people who move frequently in the forest.

A family consists of a *tinen,* or mother, a *tamen,* or father, and at least one *anak,* or child. *Tepun,* or grandparents, live in the *lamin* with the rest of the family. There are usually two to ten families in a single nomadic band.

Young children and elderly people spend all their time close to home, while the adults use the village as a base camp.

Constructing a hut: After making the frame from young trees, the family will construct a waterproof roof from palm leaves and build a grated wooden floor off the ground.

Every day men and women travel through the forest in search of food and other forest products. Sometimes they are gone for several days. Then they build *tapung,* sleeping shelters made from leaves, saplings, bamboo, and vines.

A village is usually occupied for many weeks, but it is not long before the huts begin to deteriorate and become infested with insects. The Penan move according to an unwritten plan. They know where they have recently been and where they should go to find plentiful game and sago that needs to be harvested. Each nomadic band knows the boundaries of its own

41

territory and won't stray into another band's part of the forest unless invited.

THE EMPTY PLACE

One reason a band may move is the death of a community member. When a person dies the Penan cannot bear to see the empty place left behind by their loved one. First, however, they quickly wrap the body in woven mats and bury it near the camp or under the hearth of the dead person's hut. The Penan try to soften their grief by moving and building new shelters in another part of the rain forest.

The Penan use special names when talking about people who have died. These names include the river nearest to where a person died and is buried. For example, if a woman died near the Uten River she would be referred to as *Redu Uten*, literally "female Uten." The name she was called during her life would not be mentioned again for many years.

The Penan believe in an afterlife. Their "heaven" is a rain forest above the sky where human souls hunt and harvest sago without hardship, illness, or pain.

THE SPIRIT WORLD

Traditional Penan religion is based on the belief that spirits live inside plants and animals. The forest, they believe, is filled with powerful spirits. These sometimes help the people but more often do them harm.

Ungap are the most feared spirits of all. They can hurt people, but more often they hide game, usually pigs, from hunters. The Penan believe that if the *Ungap* hear hunters talking about a hunting trip, then the hunt will fail. Therefore, the Penan avoid talking about hunting before and during a hunt. Instead of saying "we are going hunting with spears and dogs," they say *pita silat*–"we look for fan palm shoots."

THE THUNDER GOD

When the spirit of an animal, dead or alive, is angered, the Penan believe the spirit may call upon Balé Gau–the god of thunder. Balé Gau has the power to turn people to stone. While traveling through the forest the Penan often point to rock formations that they believe were once people. They say that these ancient ones were punished by the god of thunder for mocking an animal by dressing it like a human.

OMEN AND TABOO

Cutting down large, old trees is **taboo**, or prohibited. Trees are believed to have spirits that are related to the ancient ancestors. If the spirit, or *baleh,* escapes from the tree, the people will be punished.

The Penan also believe in **omens**, which are signs that predict events, either good or bad. Certain animals, usually

A family gathers around the fire in their simple lamin, *or hut.*

birds, deer, or snakes, are omen creatures. For example, if a banded kingfisher calls at the start of a journey, the Penan will turn back. They will continue their journey only if they hear the call of the crested rainbird. Other birdcalls signal a hunter to kill. The Penan believe if they disobey an omen or ignore a taboo they will experience some kind of hardship, such as illness or death.

The taboo against cutting down large trees makes construction of permanent houses impossible. Omens, too, keep the people moving throughout the forest. Although their movements are influenced by religious beliefs, the people also know they must move to protect their environment. Moving frequently prevents water sources from becoming polluted and game from being overhunted.

MEDICINE AND MAGIC

Illness and death, the Penan believe, are caused by spirits. Therefore, medicine and healing are rooted in magic.

Sometimes a person's illness is treated with medicines prepared from a wide variety of plants. These herbal remedies are used in response to certain symptoms, such as swelling, fever, or pain. Often a medicine not only relieves a symptom but also treats the cause of the ailment–such as an infection.

Other illnesses require a special healer known as the *dayung*. This healer knows how to communicate with the spirit world. The *dayung* decides how to treat a particular disease by listening to omens such as animal sounds and dreams.

The *dayung* holds ceremonies to pacify the bad spirits and banish them from the body. One evil spirit, for example, normally lives inside the trunk of the strangler fig tree, a vinelike tree that grows around another tree, eventually killing it. The task of the healer is to persuade this spirit to leave the human body and return to its usual home.

THE JUNGLE PHARMACY

Understanding Penan healing is difficult for Westerners, who do not easily connect body and spirit. In **Western medicine** doctors heal by treating the physical causes of disease, such as germs. The spiritual well-being of the person is rarely taken into consideration.

Usually regarded as superstitious, the **traditional medicine** practiced by indigenous peoples is now being studied by outsiders. Western scientists have found that understanding the healer's art is a process both difficult and time-consuming.

Westerners are, however, beginning to realize the vast potential of the rain forest for curing diseases. The forests are home to most of the plant species on earth, and native peoples have stored up a great body of knowledge about them. The Penan make medicines from more than 50 different plants. And many of these plants are used in various ways to produce a wide variety of drugs. For example, the leaves, bark, and stem of a plant called *gatimang* can be prepared to make several potent medicines and insect repellents.

LANGUAGE OF THE LAND

The Penan's knowledge of the rain forest is not restricted to plants. They also know how to find their way in the jungle by using physical features of the land, such as rivers, rocks, and cliffs. In a sense the forest itself speaks a language, marking the way of the Penan with familiar landmarks.

The Penan never developed their own written language, although one was created for them by **missionaries** in the 1970s. The Penan often communicate using sign language, called *saang*. The people poke sticks in the ground to which they attach leaves or feathers. These "message sticks" tell other Penan many things, including what food is available in the area or the news of someone's death.

Music is another form of language that unites people. When a hunter brings home a wild pig, the people dance to the rhythms of the *pagang,* a four-stringed bamboo instrument played only by women. Harps, flutes, and mouth organs add to the festivities. Everyone enjoys music, and the people often sing and even recite poetry while traveling in the forest.

The Penan do not have formal leaders or chiefs. Instead everyone has equal social and political status. This kind of **egalitarian** society works best in the challenging rain-forest environment, where cooperation, rather than competition, en-sures survival.

LAND IS LIFE

To the Penan, the land is everything. It speaks a language, it is music, it is religion, it is health, and it is family.

The culture of the Penan can be compared to a woven basket made by the limber, skilled hands of an old Penan

woman. The basket is strong, and is constructed of thousands of individual pieces of rattan to make beautiful patterns and designs.

Like the basket, the Penan culture is strong. It has been woven together by thousands of generations of people. The newest generation is connected to the past through tradition. And the many traditions are like an intricate design on the fabric of time.

If the forests are lost, there will be no rattan to weave into baskets. Without the land, there will be no Penan. Because, the Penan say, without the forests, they are empty shells with no spirits left inside.

Time to celebrate. This dancer moves to the rhythms of harp and flute as the people celebrate a successful hunt.

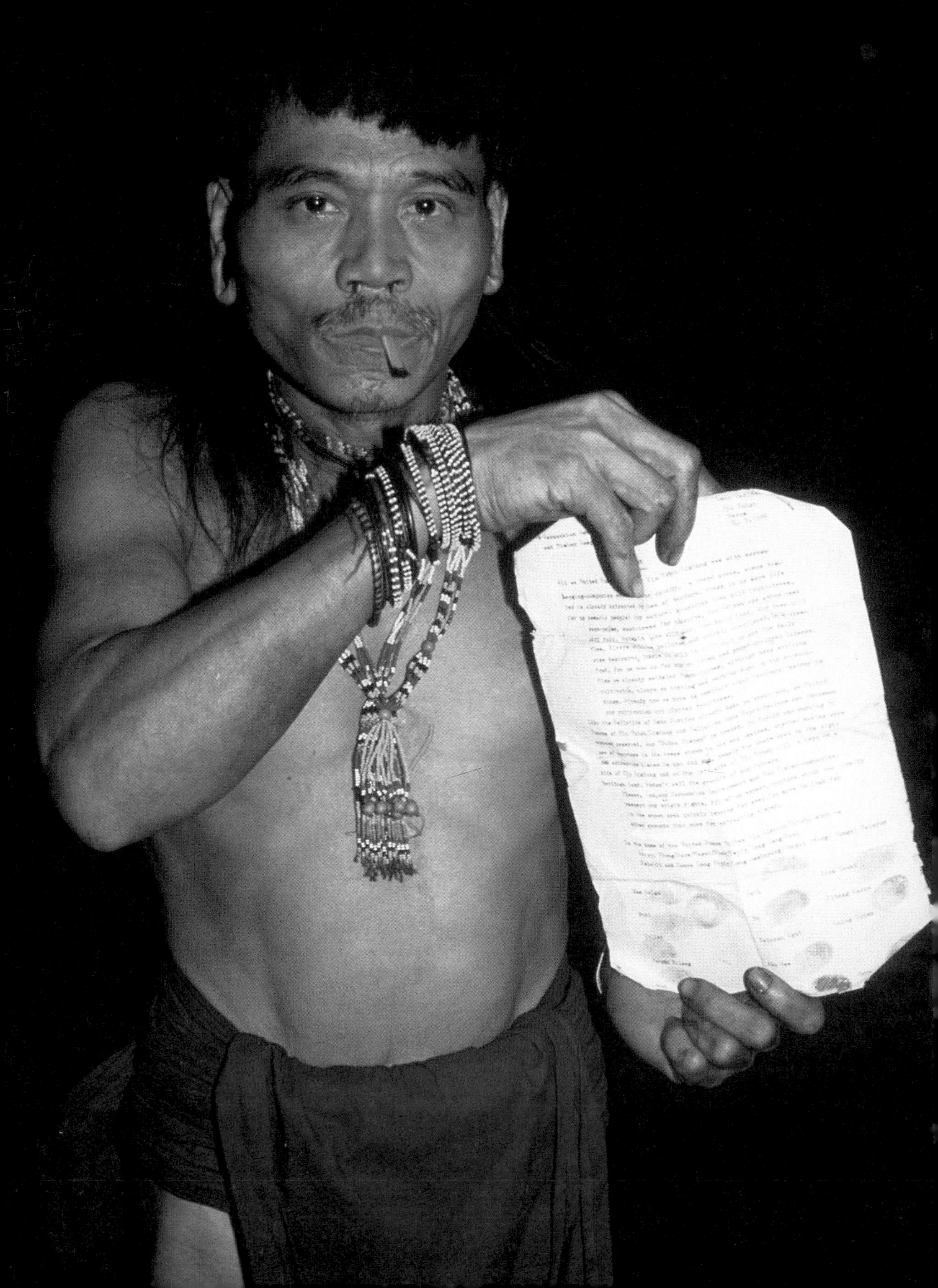

CHAPTER FOUR

THE GLOBAL VILLAGE

On a rainy afternoon, members of a Penan family rest inside their *lamin*. A fire burns on the earthen hearth and the children eagerly listen to the stories their grandmother tells. Often there is laughter as the children delight in the details of a good tale. Then the *tepun* asks the children to come closer. Now she will tell a serious story, and she asks the children to listen carefully. . . .

THE LEGEND OF THE SLOW LORIS

"Children, do you know about the small furry animal who lives high in the trees? Its eyes are wide and round, so it always looks surprised. At night it can see as well as you or I can see in the light of day. Every night it crawls through the treetops looking for fruit. It moves very slowly, barely shaking a leaf. It is so quiet that even the jungle cats have a hard time knowing it's there. By now you have probably guessed–it is the slow loris.

"One night the slow loris was sneaking through the leaves, and in the distance, hanging from a palm branch, he saw a rattan fruit. 'I want that fruit,' the slow loris whispered. Quietly and very slowly, he crept to the fruit. With his tiny hands, he snatched it from the branch.

Holding a petition to the government of Sarawak, this Penan hunter protests the destruction of his rain-forest land. The people "signed" the petition with their thumbprints.

"Now he could see that the fruit was green and felt quite firm. 'This fruit is not ripe!' said the slow loris. 'But I will not mind waiting until it is ready to eat.'

"So the slow loris held the fruit in his hands and stared at it for many days. Finally the fruit ripened and the slow loris ate it, and the juice dripped onto his fur.

"We Penan are like the slow loris. We know that if we work hard and are patient we can get what we want. We want the fruit, the game, the rattan this land gives us. We want a big piece of land kept safe from the people and machines who come to tear these forests down.

"Like the slow loris sitting in the tree–waiting, waiting–we will sit on the logging roads. We will wait, and wait, and wait, and the trucks will wait there, too, because we will be in their way.

"And then, like the slow loris, we will have a ripe fruit, too. We will have our land, our trees, our *babui,* our *uvud.* We will keep this place where our grandparents rest and where your children will be born."

PEACEFUL PROTESTS

Since 1980 the Penan and other Dayak tribes have peacefully protested against the destruction of their rain-forest homeland. At first they sent letters and petitions to the state government of Sarawak and even met with officials. But the government ignored their pleas to reduce logging in the rain forest. The Penan decided their only hope for stopping the destruction was to set up human blockades across logging roads, halting the process of trucks, bulldozers, and workers into the jungle.

Starting in March 1987, Penan families stood watch at the blockades, day and night, for eight months. The logging companies lost millions of dollars and the world took notice. Thus began an international movement to end the destruction of the Borneo rain forest.

The government responded by limiting media coverage of the protests and making the blockades illegal. Since then hundreds of Penan have been arrested and jailed.

Despite the difficulties, the Penan continue their nonviolent protests with blockades, written statements, speeches, and legal action. They say they will not give up until the destruction stops.

POLITICS AND TIMBER

Logging in Sarawak is controlled by wealthy politicians and foreign investors. The minister of forestry has the sole power to grant logging concessions, or the rights to cut timber. Often he gives concessions to other government officials and their friends and relatives.

These individuals do not cut down the trees themselves. Instead they receive big payments from logging companies in exchange for the rights to take timber. This system has made politicians, a few individuals, and the logging companies very rich.

But most of Sarawak's ordinary citizens have not benefited.

Timber companies cut the forests as quickly as possible, often working at night under floodlights. Many workers have been killed or maimed in logging accidents, but the logging never stops. The trees are not **milled** in Sarawak, but quickly loaded on to waiting ships and exported.

FOREIGN CONTROL

Sarawak sells nearly all of its trees to other countries. Japan buys most of the timber and ultimately controls much of the logging in Sarawak. Japanese banks finance logging companies, providing loans to buy heavy equipment such as bulldozers and trucks.

Beautiful smooth hardwoods, native only to the rain forest, are processed into common plywood, which is used for concrete building forms or disposable packing crates. Building forms are usually damaged after only two or three uses and then thrown into a landfill or burned. A lot of tropical hardwood is processed into cheap furniture and household items.

Turning tropical hardwoods into cheap plywood is a lot like melting gold into pennies. Japan buys tropical timber partly because it is inexpensive to import by boat from nearby Malaysia. More importantly, the logs themselves cost very little. This timber would cost much more if Sarawak **leased** areas of the rain forest directly to the timber companies and enforced environmental and safety regulations.

After petitions failed to halt the logging of their forest, the Penan set up human blockades to stop the bulldozers.

THE PENAN

Tropical hardwoods are actually cheaper to buy than low-quality, plantation-grown softwoods. Softwood is more expensive because it is grown in the United States and other northern industrial countries, where high prices are demanded.

"PROGRESS"

When criticized about the destruction of the rain forests, the government of Sarawak often replies by saying that logging brings "progress" to the "primitive people of the jungle." But the Penan have not benefited from the logging in any way.

More and more people are hungry because the shrinking forests don't produce enough game and sago. The rivers are muddy from **erosion** caused by logging, and fish are no longer plentiful.

Replacing traditional forest foods with crops is not easy for the Penan, who are used to the shade of the forest. Many people become ill when exposed to the hot sun while trying to farm land that was once rain forest.

The Penan believe they should have the right to decide what "progress" means to them. They have joined their voices with those of other Sarawak natives in a 1989 resolution:

> Some people say we are against "development" if we do not agree to move out of our land and forest. This completely misrepresents our position. Development

does not mean taking our land and forest away from us. This is not development, but theft of our land, our rights and our cultural identity. Development to us means: recognizing our land rights in practice; putting a stop to logging in our forests so we can continue to live; introducing clean water, health facilities, better schools. This kind of development we want.

CHOICES AND CHANGE

The rain-forest environment is harsh, and life there is very difficult. Tropical infections, snakebites, and the constant wet climate take a physical toll on the people. Most Penan die before they reach the age of 50. Yet while they welcome changes that make life easier, they do not want to give up their traditional way of life.

Some Penan, for example, start their campfires with cigarette lighters and hunt deer with shotguns. But these changes, insist the people, have no impact on their traditional values. They say as long as the forest remains, their culture will continue.

Some changes, however, have altered traditional beliefs. Missionaries have taught the people that obeying omens and taboos is superstition. Many Penan have given up their traditional beliefs and have accepted Christianity.

One old hunter no longer waits for an omen bird's call when setting out on a journey. This is what he told a reporter for *Time* magazine in 1991: "Before, if I went from one place to another, I had to worry about taboos. What dream did I have last night, what route should I take? Now I just go there."

But the hunter says he is sad that he no longer has dreams that ensure a successful hunt. He is sad because many young people aren't learning songs, legends, and other traditions that have been part of Penan life for generations.

A SUSTAINABLE FUTURE

The Penan know they are no longer isolated in the jungle. They are willing to accept the many challenges their community faces in the wake of rapid change. But they ask for control over a large area of land where they can pursue their way of life. They urge the government to treat the rain forest as a **renewable** natural resource-one that is carefully harvested without being destroyed. Instead of cutting down large portions of the rain forest and exporting unmilled logs, the forests could be logged selectively. The trees could then be milled by local workers and made into fine furniture, musical instruments, or other products.

A variety of alternatives to large-scale logging have been suggested. One possibility is to set aside certain areas of the forest where the Penan would harvest rattan. The products made from the rattan could then be sold widely. Garu-wood that is made into incense-is an extremely valuable forest product that could be collected and sold by the Penan.

STAY PEACEFUL

Outsiders who have lived with the Penan describe them as shy, peaceful people. They avoid conflict and settle disputes by talking things out.

Bruno Manser is an "outsider" who knows the Penan better than just about anyone. He was born and raised in Switzerland and worked as a shepherd in the Alps for ten years. His desire to learn more about himself and about the meaning of life led him to the Penan. He believed the Penan could teach him what being human is all about.

Starting in 1984, Bruno Manser lived with the Penan for six years. They accepted him fully and called him *lakeh Penan*–or a Penan person. When the bulldozers entered the forest where Manser was living, the people asked for his advice. Manser encouraged them to protest against logging. As a result, the government tried to capture Manser and attempted to shoot him. He escaped from Sarawak in 1990 and has been campaigning on behalf of the Penan ever since.

When a writer for the *New Yorker* magazine asked why he was so dedicated to saving the Penan, Manser replied, "What's being done is a violation of human rights. We are using their resources to promote our own way of life. They were a happy people, sharing everything with each other, with more than enough to eat. Their society has been in harmony with nature. *Stay peaceful* is the law of the Penan. They don't take more from

nature than they need. But look at our society. What are we leaving for future generations?"

TRIBAL WISDOM

The Penan's way of life shows their commitment to future generations. They honor the forest because it is the resting place of their ancestors, and because it provides them with everything they need. And they honor one another, understanding that community among people is more important than individual wealth or status.

In the jungle these values are never questioned. They are the truths–the tribal wisdom–that ensure the survival of the group. Perhaps the ancient wisdom and values of the Penan could benefit all people as we strive to live in harmony with the earth and with one another.

The Penan are a proud and peaceful people, determined to hold on to the traditions of their ancestors and the land of their birth.

ACTIVITIES

1. <u>Write letters on behalf of the Penan and the Borneo rain forest.</u> Government officials who receive just one letter from a concerned person think the views expressed are the same as those held by hundreds of other people who didn't take the time to write. This is why even one letter is so important. When you write, be very polite and keep your letters short. Here are some points to make in your letters:

- The national government of Malaysia and the state government of Sarawak should recognize the rights of the Penan and other Dayaks to their lands.
- Logging should be stopped on tribal lands.
- The Penan and other Dayaks shouldn't be arrested and jailed for defending their land.
- The Penan should have a say in the kind of development and changes that will affect their lives.

Send your letters to the following:

> Prime Minister of Malaysia
> Prime Minister's Department
> Jalan Dato'Onn
> 50502 Kuala Lumpur
> MALAYSIA

> Chief Minister of Sarawak
> Chief Minister's Office
> Petra Jaya, 93503 Kuching
> Sarawak, MALAYSIA

> Minister of Environment and Tourism
> Ministry of Environment and Tourism
> 8th Floor, Bangunan Tunku
> Abd. Rahmen
> Petra Jaya, 93502 Kuching
> Sarawak, MALAYSIA

Chairperson, Sarawak State Cabinet Committee
   on Penan Affairs
13th Floor, Wisma Sumber Alam
Jalan Stadium, Petra Jaya
93050 Kuching
Sarawak, MALAYSIA

Secretary-General
The United Nations
New York, NY 10017

2. <u>Boycott, or refuse to buy, products made by companies that import tropical hardwoods from the Borneo rain forest.</u> Be sure to write a letter to the president of the particular company, explaining why you no longer buy its products.

The names of companies contributing to the destruction of rain forests around the world can be obtained from:

Rainforest Action Network
450 Sansome
Suite 700
San Francisco, CA 94111

Check your local lumber yards, hardware stores, and discount stores to find out if they sell *luan*. This is the name given to processed tropical hardwood. Often it is made into cheap furniture. Ask the store managers not to sell products made from *luan*. Explain how selling products made from *luan* is destroying the rain forests.

3. <u>Send support to or join an organization that is working on behalf of the Penan and other indigenous peoples in Sarawak.</u> Below is a list of international nongovernmental organizations.

Cultural Survival
215 First Street
Cambridge, MA 02142

Endangered Peoples Project
c/o 1073 Clyde Avenue
Station A
Vancouver, British Columbia
CANADA V7T 1E3

Sahabat Alam Malaysia (SAM)
(Friends of the Earth)
P.O. Box 216
98058 Marudi
Baram, Sarawak
MALAYSIA

Society for Threatened Peoples
Bruggerstrasse 78
Baden
SWITZERLAND

Survival International
310 Edgware Road
London W2 1DY
UNITED KINGDOM

WILD
20 Water Street
Vancouver, British Columbia
CANADA V6B 1A4

World Wide Fund for Nature (WWF International)
Avenue du Mont-Blanc
1196 Gland
SWITZERLAND

4. <u>Learn about the rain forests in the United States and work to protect them.</u> When the United States criticizes foreign countries for destroying their rain forests, foreign governments often reply by saying that the U.S. government destroys its own rain forests.

There are ancient rain forests in the northwestern United States. They are not tropical rain forests because they are too far north. However, they receive just as much rain as many tropical rain forests and are also rich in biological diversity. The United States also has tropical rain forests in the Hawaiian Islands.

You can learn more about U.S. rain forests and how to protect them from these books:

Ancient Forests. Alexandra Siy. New York: Dillon Press, 1991.
Hawaiian Islands. Alexandra Siy. New York: Dillon Press, 1991.

FOR FURTHER READING

Burger, Julian. *The Gaia Atlas of First Peoples.* New York: Anchor Books, 1990.

The Earthworks Group. *50 Simple Things Kids Can Do to Save the Earth.* Kansas City: Andrews and McMeel, 1990.

Ripley, S. D. *The Land and Wildlife of Tropical Asia.* New York: Time-Life Books, 1971.

GLOSSARY

anthropologists–scientists who study groups of people, including their physical and cultural characteristics, customs, and social relationships.

biological diversity–refers to the variety of living species in an area.

canopy–the top layer of tree growth in a forest.

cassava–tropical plant that originated in South America; cultivated for its edible starchy roots.

ceding–giving up rights to a territory to another party.

colonialism–the system by which a country enters a foreign land in order to make a profit by exploiting, or using, the resources found there.

economy–a system of producing, distributing, and consuming resources and wealth.

egalitarian–based on the belief that all people should have equal political, social, and economic rights.

endemic–native to a particular region.

erosion–the washing away of soil by rain or wind. This happens when there are no tree roots or plants to hold the soil in place.

evolve–to change gradually.

geological–relating to the physical nature and history of the earth.

global village–the modern world, in which all nations communicate, share experiences, and depend on one another for resources.

indigenous–people who belong, or have traditionally lived, in an area; also called native, tribal, original, aboriginal, or first people.

latex–a milky liquid found in certain plants; it is the source of rubber.

lease–to grant the use of land for a defined purpose and for a fixed time in exchange for money.

longhouses–wooden houses built by many Dayak tribes to shelter the entire community; a longhouse is like a long string of apartments under one roof–each family has its own living space.

mill–to process trees into lumber or other wood products.

missionaries–people who are sent by their church to a foreign country to teach and convert indigenous peoples to their religious faith.

nomadic–a way of life in which people have no permanent houses but move around in search of food.

omens–things or events that are supposed to foretell the future, either good or evil.

prey–an animal that is hunted by another animal, or person, for food.

rattan–a climbing palm with long, slender, tough stems.

renewable–something that can grow back or be restored to its original condition.

resin–a substance that can be drained from certain trees and plants and used to make a variety of products, including varnishes and lacquers.

shifting cultivation–a method of growing food that involves clearing a small area of forest and cultivating it for a short time and then moving to another area when the soil in the first garden is unproductive.

species–a group of animals or plants that share many characteristics. Members of the same species can mate and have offspring.

stewardship–use and protection of the land with the goal that it will be able to provide for future generations.

taboo–something that is forbidden by tradition.

traditional medicine–long-established folk remedies that have been handed down orally through the generations; traditional medicine uses herbal cures and involves spiritual beliefs.

Western medicine–the system of medicine that seeks to understand and treat the *causes* of disease, such as germs; this contrasts with traditional medicine, which treats the *symptoms* of disease and involves spiritual aspects of health and illness.

INDEX

ABOUT THE AUTHOR

Alexandra Siy's interest in the natural world began during the first celebration of Earth Day, when she was ten years old. She studied biology in college and went on to do research in a biotechnology laboratory. Later she earned a master's degree in science education and taught high-school biology and physiology.

Ms. Siy, who lives in Albany, New York, now divides her time between writing and raising her two young children. **Global Villages** continues the theme of the interconnectedness of people and the environment, which she began in the **Circle of Life**, her first group of books for Dillon Press.